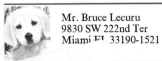
E UNITED STATES

Silly Cow

A comedy

Ben Elton

Samuel French — London
New York - Toronto - Hollywood

SILLY COW

First presented by Phil McIntyre by arrangement with Proscenium Productions Ltd at the Theatre Royal Haymarket, London, on 20th February 1991. The cast, in order of appearance, was as follows:

Sidney	Patrick Barlow
Doris	Dawn French
Peggy	Victoria Carling
Douglas	Alan Haywood
Eduardo	Kevin Allen

Directed by Ben Elton
Designed by Terry Parsons
Produced by Philip McIntyre

CHARACTERS

Sidney
Doris
Peggy
Douglas
Eduardo

The action of the play takes place in the living-room of
Doris Wallis's flat

Time: 1991

Other plays by Ben Elton
published by Samuel French Ltd

Gasping

Popcorn

ACT I

SCENE 1

Doris Wallis's flat. Morning

There is a sideboard with drinks, glasses, two candelabras, and a bowl of fruit, including grapes. There is a TV set, a sofa, and a desk covered in papers and envelopes, and holding a typewriter, a pen and a paper knife. On one of the walls, there is a mirror

Sidney sits on the sofa. He likes to think of himself as a rough diamond. He is a populist tabloid newspaper man

Sidney For Gawd's sake, Doris, pull your finger out; if you take much longer getting dressed you'll have gone out of fashion and have to start all over again.

Doris emerges from her boudoir in her expensive, gaudy dressing-gown (kimono style), putting finishing touches to her hair. She is a big, bold, brassy, witty, women's features journalist; she has her own TV comment column which is pure abuse

Doris Sidney, Sidney, Sidney, there may be cameras. You have to imagine what you're going to look like in the bitchy photo bit of some Sunday mag: "Doris Wallis knew it would be curtains for her in court, so she decided to wear a pair..." The skirt might take a while, I'm afraid. Tight little black number, bought in a spirit of optimism, it's like trying to get a space-hopper into a gumboot.

Doris retreats into her boudoir

Sidney I must say this business of taking the press to court is becoming rather worrisome. Actresses, novelists, that murderer's missus. Where will it end? "Is the press to be shackled by an unhealthy obsession with the facts?" we ask ourselves. It's going to make for some very dull breakfast reading if everything we write has to be true.

Doris emerges fully dressed

Doris Well, what do you think?

Sidney My darling, you look like mutton dressed as a rat.

Doris So you've been reading my new Fergie piece then.

Sidney Beautiful bit of work, like watching a mugging. That's why you should be working for me. The stuff is poetry, wasted on your current editor; the clueless arse will probably print it upside down in the sports page.

Doris He won't be printing it at all at the moment; I can't copy it through, my modem's down... This junk was supposed to make our lives simpler! Let me tell you, I've never had a postman go down on me.

Sidney Well, quite. Tell you what, if you print it up, I'll fax it through for you on the trusty portable.

Doris Peggy does my admin, thank you, Sidney.

Sidney Fair enough.

Doris I shall put my trust in a simple envelope... A couple of days won't matter either way, this piece is timeless. "Poor fatty Fergie looked like an explosion in a pizza factory. Either the Duchess of Pork has gone psychedelic or young Beatrice had just been sick."

Sidney Like I said, poetry. You really are a nasty woman, my darling, creeping about making other people's lives a misery. The world lost a great traffic warden the day you opted for features journalism.

Doris It's a dirty job but somebody has to do it. I'm the nasty cow who slaughters the sacred cows. Please feel free to have another bucket of Scotch. I'm going to finish my face.

Doris exits

Sidney Doris, darling. Believe it or not I do try and do a bit of work between drinks. Starting a new paper from scratch does require a modicum of time and commitment, especially if you've been away as long as I have. Nobody knows me in the UK any more and I have rather a lot to prove... So if you'll just sign this letter of intent then I can...

Doris (*off*) Sidney, I haven't time... (*She snorts loudly*)

Sidney Call me old-fashioned, Doris, but I could have sworn you were supposed to put the powder on your nose not up it.

Doris emerges perkily

Doris Looking good is about feeling good, Sidney.

Sidney Yes, well, I'd feel a great deal better with something a little more concrete to show my publishers. Bugger my boots, Doris, this is my break! English language editor of the first Euro tabloid! Think of it! Kelvin MacKenzie they could have asked, Derek Jameson, Larry Lamb, anyone, but no, they sent to America for little old nobody Sid!

Doris Well, pardon me if I don't chew your trousers off right now and kiss the great man's bum.

Sidney Doris!

Doris I've said I'll probably take the job and I really don't see why I should have to sign anything.

Sidney Three months I have courted you, my love, it's three long months since I wrote you from the States! I've got through entire marriages in less time than that.

Doris I just have a problem with signing things, that's all. I think I must have been scared by a contract as a small child.

Sidney Don't you trust me?

Doris Of course I trust you, Candyfloss. I trust all editors to be dirty, duplicitous little weasels and not one has ever failed me.

Sidney Doris, I have given up everything for this project.

Doris You're not the only one who'll be giving things up, Sidney Skinner! You're not the only one who's had to work hard for everything they've got! While you were sneaking around Hollywood trying to buy photos of Jackie Onassis with her fun bags flying, I was dogsbody on the *Preston Clarion*, and I mean dogsbody.

Sidney We all did our time in births and funerals, Doris.

Doris Yes, and I'm never going back. These last few years I've finally got a grip of *la dolce vita* and I'm sticking my talons in deep. I am never again going to get up at five thirty on a rainy morning to report on a sheep-dog trial, I am never again going to cover the Liberal candidate in a by-election, and I am never again going to review another show at Preston Rep...

Sidney Doris, this is all very interesting but...

Doris There was this appalling old ham; I'd watched him every three weeks for two and a half years, and whatever part he played, he did his Noël Coward impression. Hamlet's ghost, Noël Coward. *The Crucible*, Noël Coward; *Mother Courage*, Noël Coward. Imagine what the old fart was like when he actually had to play in a Noël Coward—his accent got so clipped I swear he was only using the first letter of each word. So please believe me, Sidney, I am never going back to that. I've done my time, Sidney, and now it's paying off. I've got my own column, I've cooked with Rusty on TV-AM, two *Blankety Blank*s last series, and Les called me Cuddles. What's more, tonight is the big one, I get my first *Wogan*. These are not things you throw away lightly, Sidney. Which is why I am just a little bit hesitant about ending up in Stuttgart working for an editor I scarcely know.

Sidney Look, you're right to be cautious, Doris, but this is just a non-binding letter of intent to impress the krauts. I need something firm.

Doris And as far as I'm concerned your krauts can shove something firm up their collective lederhosen. I don't like being pushed around and I certainly wouldn't dream of signing anything without showing it to Peggy.

Sidney Gawd knows what you think you gain by showing it to Peggy anyway. You should be showing it to a lawyer.

Doris If Peggy thinks it's necessary, she'll show it to a lawyer.

Sidney She worries me that one. I can't say as I like her over much. She's a bit sly, two-faced.

Doris Sidney, if Peggy had two faces I doubt she'd be wearing the sourpuss one she wears at the moment. Anyway I don't want you to like my staff. They're not there for you to like them. Now can you please shut up about Peggy, the letter, and the firmness of your krauts while I get ready for this bloody court case.

Sidney Well, if you really want to know, I reckon that jacket's a bit much for Judge Jeffries.

Doris Which just goes to show that you are a tasteless old tart and wouldn't recognize a good thing if it sat on your face and farted up your nose... These jugs are worth a character reference from the Archbishop of Canterbury. Not sexy, you see, jolly. Anyway, it'll have to do, I'm not going to change again. Where the hell are my notes...?

Sidney Well, judging by the way you run your life, I presume Miss Piggy will have them.

Doris I don't even know where the bloody court is. If she doesn't get here soon, knockers or no knockers, we shall lose this case by default...

Sidney You rely on that girl far too much. She'll get poached by some Channel Four lefty who doesn't think it's a compromise to have a servant as long as he calls her a PA.

Doris Lose Peggy? Don't, I wouldn't know where my arse was to wipe it.

Sidney You're a sculptor, Doris, and the English language is your clay.

Doris Thank you.

We hear the sound of the front door slamming, a loud "So-rry", and Peggy rushes in, briefcase and bag in hand. She has rather severe brunette hair and is efficiently, if slightly dowdily, dressed

Peggy Sorry—that latch still isn't catching, you know, any manner of nasty type could just walk right in.

Sidney I think one just did.

Doris Peggy, where the hell have you been?! This is a bloody important day.

Peggy Doris, I don't believe it. The car will be here in half an hour, Douglas is coming around to get the accounts signed, we still haven't got back to that *Wogan* researcher about tonight's show, and you haven't even changed.

Sid laughs

Doris Peggy, this is my court gear. Just because you choose to dress like you're applying for a mortgage. I am dressed to win. That bitch will take one look at these glad rags and confess to murdering Lord Lucan.

Sidney Of course she will... Hallo, Peggy.

Peggy Good morning, Mr Skinner.

Doris Don't call him "Mister", Peggy, it gives him airs. The man doorsteps queer newsreaders for a living.

Sidney We perform a valuable social service, my darling. After all, surely the public has a right to know which of its newsreaders are queer!

Doris Well, of course it does, Sidney! The right to doorstep queer newsreaders is a cornerstone of our precious democracy! Take away that freedom and what have you got? *Pravda*, that's what!

Sidney Well, quite. Anyway, Peggy, I've been oiling round your beautiful boss for three months now. I think you and I can insult each other on first name terms, eh? Go on, defrost that grimace, call me Sidney.

Peggy Yes, but if the deal collapses and Doris decides she doesn't want to be your Euro features editor, that's when I think "Mr Skinner" would be more businesslike.

Sidney Well, you are certainly a cool one, aren't you?

Doris Cool? Peggy can freeze a man at twenty paces; I swear sometimes when she opens her mouth a light comes on.

Sidney Well, let me tell you, Doris, if you're thinking of letting her talk you into pulling this deal after I've spent three months with my tongue so far up your backside I know how many fillings you've got...

Doris Oh, for pity's sake! Look, Peggy... Sidney wants me to sign this. He says it contains nothing binding.

Sidney Of course it doesn't, it is simply a polite bloody note to a consortium of Huns who are considering paying you *mucho* marks and loadsa lira to say that you might be interested in becoming their resident Eurobitch. You are not committed, you are not bound, you will not wake up tomorrow to find *The Time Life History of the American Civil War* on your doorstep. All it does is give another little building block with which to assemble the deal.

Doris Peggy?

Peggy Mr Skinner's right, it's pretty innocuous, but I still wouldn't sign it, Doris. Why should you? If your present boss saw it...

Sidney Present boss? What's your present boss got to do with anything? I was under the impression, Doris, that your present boss is about to become your ex-boss.

Doris Oh, just give it here... Eyebrow pencil do?

Sidney I think not. Blood would be acceptable.

Doris Peggy, pen. There, satisfied?

Sidney Satisfied? I don't think I'd go that far. Let us just say that for the time being I have returned the pills and the razor blade to the bathroom cupboard. (*He goes to the sideboard to pour himself a drink*)

Peggy Um, Mr Skinner, Doris and I have business to discuss and her car will be here at twelve to take her to court. I don't want to rush you…

Sidney You won't, my darling, you won't. (*He pours himself a drink*)

Doris Twelve, Peggy! But we have to pick up Eduardo!

Peggy Eduardo is being picked up first, he'll be in the car.

Sidney Eduardo? Would that be the moody young fellow who was slouching on the sofa, grunting and absent-mindedly readjusting his wedding tackle last time I visited?

Doris It would, and so what?

Sidney I really don't think taking him to court is much of an idea, Doris. This toy boy thing of yours is rather naff. He can't be more than twelve.

Doris Eduardo is twenty-one years old and we are very much an item. If he's on my arm coming out of discos but not beside me in my hour of travail, it's going to make me look a bit of a sad old bag, isn't it?

Sidney If you think that the presence of a preening little juvenile delinquent with a courgette in his trousers is going to help your case, you don't know British justice.

Doris Sweetheart, you have got your letter.

Sidney Just finishing the old slurp.

Doris Well, leave Eduardo out of this.

Sidney All I'm saying is that, if you hear a gentle thud during the judge's summing-up, don't bother to look round—it will be Eduardo's balls dropping.

Doris Sidney, do your Teutonic employers want a columnist, or do they want a celebrity columnist?

Sidney Doris, fame is the spur.

Doris Right, well, toy boys are the price you pay for a happening image like mine, so why don't you conserve your stupendous wit for the next waitress you are trying to impress, and let Peggy and me concentrate for one minute on this bloody case.

Sidney Fair enough.

Peggy (*taking a newspaper cutting out of her briefcase*) I phoned your brief again this morning and he says it could go either way. People are rather turning against the excesses of the press. Since the Cornwell business there's been Jeffrey Archer and Elton John and any number of…

Doris Excesses! Give me that. (*She grabs the clipping, quoting*) Look, here it is, Sidney: "What, oh, what makes that silly cow Trudi Hobson think she can act?" and "Was it a feminist statement to give the part to such a total dog?"…

Sidney A robust but acceptable critique.

Doris Good-natured, two-fisted, popular copy… (*She continues to read*) "Those huge, wobbling, quilted thighs, jammed up against the hem of her hot pants like two great, pink, floppy draught-excluders, made one pray for liposuction on the National Health…"

Sidney Fair criticism.

Doris Bold, brassy stuff. I just don't see the problem.

Peggy I think she was hurt.

Doris Hurt! My mother brought up five kids on a widow's pension.

Peggy Now, that's not actually true, Doris.

Doris Well, somebody's mother did. I cannot imagine what induced the silly cow to take offence!

Peggy (*taking the papers*) As you well know, Doris, the centre of her case, apart from disputing the claim that she has concave breasts, and gargantuan love-handles, is the professional slur. You said she couldn't act. She's pushing the detrimental-to-her-employment thing hard, and six months out of work has added to her claim. You must take it seriously.

Doris I love it when you're firm with me, Peggy. She's terribly pretty when she's firm, isn't she, Sidney?

Peggy Doris, please. The case.

Doris I said she couldn't act; Christ, if Roger Moore had been able to act, do you think he'd be the star he is today?

Peggy Look, you really mustn't be flippant like this in court, Doris; the woman's a wreck, she's lost everything over this case. She was highly respected and you said... "What with the disappearance of the rain forests, it was ecologically unsound of the Beeb to use such a wooden actress."

Doris But I say that sort of thing about everyone, I am the "Ratbag of the Ratings". Nothing is sacred—invalids, children; I once single-handedly destroyed a kid's career.

Peggy Doris, it's not relevant...

Doris Absolutely turned him into a national joke. This repulsive, simpering little pre-pubescent tick, looked like a bloody girl. Never stopped working, Dickens' musicals, kids' adventures, became a sort of national pet...

Peggy Doris, we have to concentrate.

Doris I thought, "Right, my lad, I shall string you up by your first pubic hair". He did these ravioli ads, grinning away saying, "I wanta some more, Mama", sucking up great mounds of the stuff, sounded like oral sex in the elephant house. Every week for a month I made a little joke about it. They ended up having to ditch the campaign.

Sidney God knows, Doris, I hope she doesn't win. You've had poison in your pen for half a decade, you could be going to court from now till Domesday. I saw the clippings in America, they're dripping with blood. That bit you did about the New, New Saint, I'm sure his lunchbox would satisfy a starving mouse ... and the piece saying that bloke's Geordie accent, in the Bleasdale, had arrived on Tyneside via Pakistan.

Doris Look, I said she couldn't bloody act and she had a couple of whopping great thunder thighs. I'm not a serious critic, everybody knows that, I'm a bitch; my TV page is a column, people read it for the bitching.

Peggy The problem is, of course, the woman can actually act a bit—

Grotowski, Peter Brook, *Morecambe and Wise Christmas Show*; a season
at the RSC.

Sidney Yes, she even came over and did her Juliet and all that bollocks for
us in the States.

Peggy And you can be certain she'll bring that up today.

Doris Oh, and I suppose just because some bunch of over-subsidized, toffee-
nosed, bulgie brains happen to appreciate her classical enunciation, our six
and a half million readers have to grovel to superior beings, is that it?

Peggy I think this is definitely one of your strongest cards. Our lawyer says
the judge we've got will love the anti-intellectual bit; if she starts claiming
a definitive Desdemona she's in trouble.

Sidney The common touch, that's the way to play it.

Doris Of course it is, people actually like my stuff, unlike the almighty RSC
which people only pretend to like. We don't need a couple of million a year
scrounged off the government to stay afloat.

The door intercom buzzer sounds

Oh, God, that can't be Eduardo yet!

Peggy I think it will be Douglas… (*She moves to the intercom*)

Sidney And who's Douglas, my dear? Surely not another pouting little three-
year-old dago to lend emotional credibility to your case?

Peggy (*into the intercom*) Hallo? … Mr Robertson. Please do come on up.

Doris Douglas is my accountant, Sidney…

Sidney Ah ha, an accountant, eh? A wolf in shit's clothing.

Doris He's a decent bloke, Sidney. It'll be a new experience for you.

Sidney And how would you know that he's a decent bloke? He didn't tell
you so himself by any chance, did he?

Peggy I told her so, Mr Skinner.

Sidney Now, did you really, Peggy, so you're a financial expert as well as
a legal one, are you?

Peggy I took advice from Ms Wallis's bank manager, her agent, her solicitor
and independent advisors…

Sidney And no doubt came up with some Brylcreemed super yuppy with a
portable phone strapped to his dick.

There is a knock at the door

Peggy Just push it, Douglas, the latch is faulty. (*She opens the door*)

*Outside is Douglas Robertson. He is a dignified old gentleman, leather
patches on sleeves, ancient leather briefcase. A kindly, but astute old
fellow*

Doris Enter the yuppy.

Peggy Hallo, Mr Robertson.

Douglas Good morning, Peggy, my dear. How very lovely to see you.

Doris Hallo, Douglas, it's a long way up, you must be knackered; come and sit down.

Douglas It's thoughtful of you, Doris. Gravity does appear to exert something of a greater pressure on me than in years gone by.

Peggy takes his coat

Thank you, Peggy. I'm sure that Newton missed a trick when he failed to equate increases in gravitational pull with advancing years.

Doris He'd have spotted it quick enough if he'd been a woman, Douglas; I'll tell you, without a couple of RSJs under these, (*she indicates her bust*), I'd be polishing my shoes with them.

Sidney Nobody puts it like you put it, Doris.

Douglas I don't believe I've had the pleasure, sir...

Sidney Good thing too at your age. (*He laughs a friendly laugh*) Sidney Skinner, Doug, Doris's new boss.

Doris Prospective boss, Sidney.

Sidney Have it your own way, precious. Well, here's to the lot of you. (*He drinks*) Now, then, Doris, I know your diary's about as crowded as the M25, so I'll just take my letter and get out of your short and curlies...

Peggy Um, Doris, I was wondering if, before Mr Skinner goes, it might not be a good idea to let Mr Robinson take a look at the letter you signed for him. You know, just as a kind of ... second opinion.

Sidney (*hating Peggy*) Darling, that is mine and Doris's affair and none other's. Besides, as I keep telling you, it's only a letter of intent. It is non-bloody-binding.

Doris In which case, what's the problem?

Sidney There isn't a problem! I just happen to believe in the rights of privacy, that's all.

Doris I shall remember that when you ask me to stake out Elton John's bog.

Doris exits to her boudoir

Sidney (*pompously*) The lavatories of the famous are news, Doris, it's completely different.

Douglas Is this letter something you've signed, Doris? You really must be most careful about things which you are called on to sign.

Sidney And what business is it of yours, mate?

Douglas Excuse me, sir, but Doris's business is my business, I am her accountant.

Sidney Exactly. A bloody ledger filer.

Douglas It is an honourable profession.

Sidney Honourable profession? What? Convincing the Revenue she spends a grand a week on pencils and Tippex. Listen, Doris, this letter has nothing to do with...

Douglas (*quietly very angry*) Neither your letter nor your affairs interest me in the slightest, sir. I am here simply to complete Miss Wallis's accounts.

Sidney (*conciliatory*) Well, of course you are. I didn't mean to be personal. I'll tell you what, if you're interested, I've just come back from donkey's years in the States and I've got a fairly substantial but rather dodgy pile hanging around off shore...

Douglas It is quite clear to me the type of accountant that you favour, Mr Skinner. The type who supervised Doris's affairs until she came to me.

Doris enters

Doris Always have a straight accountant, Sidney. If you've got the dosh you can get away with most things in this country, but one thing Her Majesty won't stand for is not getting her cut. I can't think of anyone better placed to give us an honest opinion on your nasty little non-binding letter than Douglas... (*She grabs the envelope from Sidney*) Would you mind, Douglas? (*She hands it to Douglas*) Thank you.

Sidney Yes, by all means take a look, Douglas, and then perhaps Peggy would like to have the bloody thing published in *The Times* so that everybody can get a sneak preview of our plans.

Doris Oh, don't be such a drama queen, Sidney.

Douglas Well, as Mr Skinner has so rightly pointed out, I am only an accountant, but even to my layman's eyes this document appears to be entirely innocent.

Sidney Thank you.

Douglas From the brief perusal I have made, it seems to be no more than a vague statement of possible future interest in a Pan-European publishing venture. (*He returns the envelope to Doris's desk*)

Doris Thank you, Douglas. Better safe than sorry, Sidney.

Sidney Well, you may rest assured that your new and loving boss will be going through your expenses with a nit comb once I've got you in my horrible clutches.

Doris Goodbye, Sidney.

Sidney Understood, a nod's as good as a wink. (*Draining his glass, he crosses to the table. To Peggy*) And speaking of expenses, Peggy, let me assure you that personal assistants are not claimable. (*He snatches up the envelope from the crowded desk and makes for the door*)

Peggy Goodbye, Mr Skinner.

The buzzer rings again

Sidney Perhaps that's the milkman, perhaps Peggy would like me to show
him the letter for a quick once over, just to be sure. After all, his brilliant
milkman's eye may spot something sinister that a simple accountant might
miss.

Peggy (*into the intercom*) Hallo? What? But you're miles too early ... oh,
well, you'd better come up. (*She puts down the intercom*) It's Eduardo.

Sidney Oh, my Gawd, phone the society for the prevention of cruelty to
children. Madam's jail-bait has arrived.

Peggy I'm sorry about this, Doris, I distinctly told him twelve o'clock.

Sidney He probably needs his nappy changing.

Doris Sidney, hilarious though this paedo gag is, I consider it a touch rich
coming from somebody who is going to be regularly exposing some poor
sixteen-year-old bimbo's bazookas Europe-wide simply to provide Joe,
Jacques and Juan public with the stimulus they require for their Euro
stiffies.

Sidney (*pompously*) The fun-loving photos in my newspapers will be there
to express a joyful appreciation of the fulsome beauty of the youthful
female form.

Doris Sidney, they're there to help people wank.

Douglas (*very embarrassed*) Uhm ... perhaps I've called at an inconvenient
time...

Doris Well, you're here now, so don't worry about it.

There is a knock at the door. Peggy opens it

*Eduardo stands outside. He is about twenty. A handsome, cocky, streetwise,
male bimbo. He carries a bunch of flowers*

Eduardo (*walking straight to Doris*) He's here! Hallo, beautiful, what's
shaking? Wicked little number, totally rockin'. I like a bit of purple. Wear
it for me?

Sidney Honestly, Doris, he'll have to go. See you.

Sidney leaves

Doris Eduardo, what the hell are you doing here...?

Peggy The car was supposed to pick you up at twelve.

Eduardo Came early dinnit. Aren't you pleased to see me? Had me barnet
done special. (*He checks his hair in the mirror, pleased*) Murder or what?
Raving, as it happens. Twenty-three notes, you can't knock it. Here's your
good luck flowers... Hope you like them, you paid for them.

Doris Peggy, do something creative with these, please.
Peggy Of course. I'll put them in water, there's some in the lavatory.

Douglas clears his throat

Doris Oh yes, excuse me, Douglas, this is Eduardo, he's a friend of mine.
Douglas Good morning, Eduardo.
Eduardo Murder, Doug, happening. You one of Doris's toy boys then? Ha ha ha.
Doris Douglas is my accountant, sweetie. Like you, he has to juggle with large and slightly unmanageable figures, but there the resemblance ends. Now then, sugar plum, Douglas and I have a bit of business to go over so you just sit tight and Peggy will make you a little drinkie.
Eduardo Awesome. Er, tequila, Peggs. Actually I've got a bit of business for you myself, Doris.
Peggy Tequila, Eduardo? You have to be in court in an hour.
Eduardo Yeah, gonna be a banging good rave innit? Hope the judge has got a big wig, they're classic them wigs. Tasty or what? I went to court before, chillin' it was, we'd had E so we was wasted, but it wasn't really funny 'cos this Richard I knew got five years. Wish we could have stopped giggling 'cos he was a mate.
Peggy Small tequila then? (*She goes up to fix a drink*)
Douglas Five years! Good lord, Eduardo, what had your friend done?
Eduardo I told you. He was a Richard.
Doris Peggy, Eduardo's drink quite quickly, please.
Douglas But being called Richard isn't a crime.
Eduardo No, the geezer dealt, Doug. He sold gear. Richard, Richard Gere, dealer, you thick or what? He sold...
Doris (*quickly*) I agree with you Douglas, it does seem rather a harsh sentence for impersonating a film star.
Eduardo Happening! Here, Dougy boy, have a look at this, eh? (*He crosses over and shows Douglas his wrist watch*) Solid gold Rolex. Top watch. Murder innit? Two grand.
Douglas It looks very ... uhm ... reliable.
Eduardo I'll tell you what, mate, it's reliable bollocks, that's what, ha ha ha. Forty notes. Bangkok, totally rockin'. Have you ever been to Bangkok, Dougy boy? They've got chicks out there who can fire darts out their foufous...
Doris Would you excuse me for a moment, Douglas?
Douglas Of course, Doris. (*Rather embarrassed, he takes papers out of his briefcase and buries himself in his work*)

Doris beckons Eduardo over, tough and intimidating

Doris Eddie?

Eduardo What's shakin'?

Doris Excuse me. (*She points at his mouth*) This is your mouth. (*She points at his crotch*) This is your brain. The distance between them is too far for a coherent thought to travel. So if you wish to continue drinking tequila and Hoovering up mirrors at my expense, you will not attempt to bridge the gap.

Eduardo (*slightly unconvincing bravado*) Keep wishing, girl. You need me because I'm happening.

Doris Eduardo, let me tell you an important fact of life. There are more penniless, loose little boys in the world than there are rich, single women. It's a buyers' market, sonny, and you're for sale. So back in your box.

Eduardo (*shaken but still attempting bravado*) Oh yeah, I get you things you need...

He produces an envelope and speaks the following to the room. Peggy and Douglas are studiously ignoring them

Like, the newspaper clippings you asked for, you'll love them, they're fresh... (*Conspiratorially to Doris*) Although some of the lines in them will get right up your nose, ha ha ha.

Doris grabs the envelope

Now say you don't love me.

Doris Eddie, this stuff is just like you. A cheap thrill, extremely common, and very easily purchased. Now then, Douglas, what can I do you for?

Douglas Well, I'm rather worried about... (*He looks at Eduardo*)

Doris Oh, you can say your piece in front of Eduardo, Douglas, he thinks a right-hand column is something to do with the way your trousers hang.

Douglas Well, it's merely your VAT accounts, they have taken some considerable effort, for which, sadly, I shall have to invoice you, but I think I've got them straight. They merely require your signature and I shall be able to pop them in an envelope and send them to the Custom and Excise people...

Doris Everybody wants my siggy today. Where do I sign?

Douglas Well, I'd rather like to take you through them before you sign, Doris. One's financial affairs are not, after all, to be taken lightly.

Eduardo Here, Peggy, did you know I can do a Kylie medley in burps?

Doris Ed, mouth open, should be shut. Douglas, don't make me try to understand money, I love it too deeply, I love it with a passion, I want to sleep with it and have its babies. How can you ask me to see it as nothing more than columns, numbers and decimal points? Would you have asked Romeo to become Juliet's gynaecologist?

Peggy Perhaps if you left them with us, Mr Robertson, Doris can go over them later and then I can get them biked round to you.
Douglas Posting will be quite sufficient, Peggy. I confess this current vogue for entrusting one's every communication to some leather-clad Apache on a motorcycle leaves me rather cold. I would happily trade a day's delay in my affairs for the comforting sight of an English postman labouring up my path and laying his honest hand on my box.
Doris Well, naturally.
Douglas Since I know that you have a trying day ahead of you, Doris, I shall wish you the very best of luck in court.
Doris Thank you and good luck with your postman.
Douglas Thank you, Peggy ... and um, goodbye, Eduardo.
Eduardo (*nearly ignoring him*) Yeah, classic, Dougy, banging.
Douglas (*at a loss*) Yes, well...

Peggy moves to the door with Douglas

Peggy (*at the door*) Thank you, Douglas, we'll be in touch.

Douglas leaves

Doris All right, Eduardo, go and wait in the car.
Eduardo Haven't finished my drink.

Doris crosses to him, grabs the drink

Doris Bottoms up, my darling. You shouldn't drink so much anyway, it destroys the brain cells, which are not something you can afford to squander lightly. Now, go and wait in the car.
Eduardo (*sullenly*) Yeah, well, I was going anyway, wasn't I. I'm just so wasted. Ravin' night last night.

He slouches out

Doris Sid's right, that one has to go.
Peggy Where on earth did you get him?
Doris Oh, he oiled his way up to me in some disco or other a couple of months ago. Luke-warm coffee, Pegs?
Peggy No thanks, Doris. I'll stick with my ginseng.
Doris Maniac. They all know good old Doris will buy them a few drinks and dust their nostrils. Don't know why I do it really; image, I suppose.
Peggy It isn't a particularly nice image, Doris.
Doris Yes, well, rather more acceptable than my real tastes, I think. The

honest British housewife appreciates me standing up for womankind, but if she were to discover that I have been known to lie down with womankind, it would be something different altogether. Something, I fear, which would not go down too well with the ironing.

Peggy No, I suppose you're probably right.

Doris You see, it's different for gay girls. The media does at least have a place for camp, cosy, cuddly old puffs, in their fluffy jumpers. I'm not saying it's easy or pleasant, but there is a sort of niche. I think a cheeky lesbian would be rather more difficult to market, don't you? "It's just after eight o'clock and time to go over to Doris the dyke with this morning's fashion tips"... It wouldn't work you see, the "top knobs" would object.

Peggy I suppose they would.

Doris Of course they would. Men as a sex fancy themselves so much they just can't imagine anybody not fancying them.

Peggy But really, Doris, Eduardo? It's a pretty unpleasant cover story. I mean rather a high price to pay.

Doris Well, I don't sleep with him, do I? You silly cow. Anyway I like having bimbos to push around. People wouldn't think twice if I was a bloke and Eduardo was a dolly bird.

Peggy I wasn't prying, Doris... I mean obviously I know what you... I mean, how you ... well, the way you...

Doris Of course you do, Peggy... (*Casually*) After all, it takes one to know one, doesn't it?

Peggy What?

Doris Well, doesn't it?

Peggy I... I don't know what you're talking about.

Doris I think you do... Anyway, better sign these accounts, get them out of the way.

Peggy Aren't you going to check them?

Doris What do you think I pay Douglas for? (*She takes up a pen*)

Peggy I'll read them through if you like...

Doris signs the accounts

Doris Too late. You may, at your leisure, bung them in an envelope and bike, post, or spiritually channel them back to dear old Douglas... Honestly, Peggy, what a morning! Sid gets worse, doesn't he? I mean, doesn't he? When God was making tosspots he certainly rolled his sleeves up for Sid.

Peggy He does grate a bit I suppose.

Doris I thank my lucky stars that the chances of me actually having to take his nasty little job in Stuttgart are pretty slim.

Peggy I do have to say, Doris, that I can't quite see the need to be so enthusiastic with Sid. If you're really not thinking of taking his job why do you encourage him so much?

Doris It's an insurance policy, Peggy, a second option. You never know, my telly plans might fall through, I certainly don't want to end up stuck in my present job.

Peggy Oh, but they won't fall through, your ideas are wonderful... I finished typing up the treatment yesterday, I left it on the desk there in an envelope.

Doris You may think my ideas are wonderful, Peggy. I certainly do, but unfortunately neither of us are commissioning editors at Channel Four and you just can't tell with Channel Four. They keep saying they want to go populist, but somehow they just can't resist those cartoons from Poland. That's why I'm stringing Sid along, just in case the telly falls through.

Peggy Not really very ethical, Doris.

Doris Please, Peggy, I'm going to cop enough character assassination in court.

Peggy Yes, and speaking of which, you really must take it seriously, Doris. The thighs are definitely going to be a problem.

Doris Why?

Peggy Well the simple facts of the matter are that she couldn't (*she refers to the notes*) "tuck them into the top of her socks".

Doris But we went through all this with the lawyer. God knows how many months ago.

Peggy Six and a half, I was still temping for the agency.

Doris Don't know what I did without you, love... As I explained at the time, if these people set themselves up they should expect to be shot down. The bitch was asking for it.

Peggy The question is, does accepting a role in a television drama series constitute asking to be called a silly, talentless, fat old cow.

Doris As far as I'm concerned it does. Yes.

Peggy I do wish I had your strength of purpose, Doris, I really do.

Doris Well, I have a simple philosophy, Peggy, my love. When the dogs are eating the dogs, you have to make damn sure that you're the biggest bitch at the table.

Peggy Well, it's all right for you, Doris, but some of us don't find it that easy. (*She bustles about getting Doris's stuff together*) Is this your court bag, Doris?

Doris Yes.

Peggy I'm all right with accounts and business things, I can hide behind a schoolmistress pose and pretend to be tough dealing with old Sid, but real life's a bit more difficult to cope with. Just coming here today, for instance, there were three men hanging off the scaffolding. I mean it's not as if I'm exactly flaunting it, is it? "Beautiful arse, love, a smile wouldn't kill you though", two thoughtless seconds for those buggers and I spend the next two hours seething with fury.

Doris I'll tell you what you have to do when that happens, Peggy. You must be nice and sweet, never sink to their level. You have to look up, give him a lovely smile, a little wiggle and then you say, (*with a big sweet smile*) "Fuck off and die, peanut prick".

Peggy God, you're a hard nut, Doris. I really do admire that.

Doris I'm the hardest, Peggy. Bogeymen get scared at night imagining me under their beds. Listen, if people start bullying you, Peggy, you tell me, all right? (*She pats her hand and holds it*)

Peggy All right, Doris.

Pause. There is a moment where more might be said between them. But the phone rings. Peggy answers it

Hallo, this is the personal assistant to Doris Wallis ... yes, of course, a car at six, that's right ... thank you, no, she will be made-up and wearing the clothes in which she intends to appear... Thank you, goodbye... (*She puts the phone down*) That was the *Wogan* people.

Doris Oh God, *Wogan*!

A distant car horn sounds

Peggy (*checking her watch*) Eduardo's getting impatient. You're all right, Doris, it isn't quite twelve yet. Are you scared?

Doris Scared, woman, don't be absurd. (*She puts on her coat*) I shall return without a stain on my character or my underwear.

Peggy Aren't you just a little bit sorry for this silly woman? I am a bit.

Doris Good. Good, because it's when other people are feeling sorry that I'm at my happiest, Peggy. I have to be, I'm a journalist, I have to be pleased when other people are sad.

Peggy (*with a nervous laugh*) You do enjoy cynicism, don't you, Doris?

Doris I'm not being remotely cynical, I'm stating the obvious. I remember exactly the first time I realized the truth about my job... There was a bomb, you see, unexploded, and I knew I wanted it to go off.

Peggy Oh, Doris, you didn't.

Doris Of course I did. All of us poor runny-nosed hacks did. We'd stood waiting for hours. If it didn't go off, what would we have to show for a day's work? Nothing. Then it did go off and we were pleased.

Peggy Yes, but you weren't actually pleased.

Doris Peggy, I was delighted. It was a particularly good bomb too. It killed a little boy and a little girl...

Peggy (*upset*) Doris, please, you don't mean that!

Doris Peggy, if nobody dies, the article's on page six. I'm on page six. What do you want me to tell you? That I hope I never come across a decent story? That I hope I never get a page one byline?

Peggy Well, no, news is news, it isn't wrong to want to report it...
Doris And what happens when you stop reporting news and start looking for
it? For instance, you've got your sports hero, the new footballer; my editor
wants some news: "Does he screw around? Does he beat his wife?"... So
I dig and I dig and it turns out the man is a decent bloke. What's my
reaction? It's the same as the bomb, Peggy, I'm angry, I'm frustrated, I
swear I am sat at my desk wishing that a man beat his wife!! That isn't very
nice, is it, Peggy?
Peggy Well, no but...
Doris No, it isn't. I know how tough I have to be to do my job. I know I
certainly do not require hysterical self-indulgent actresses getting a judge
to run it in. (*She puts on a scarf*) I'll see you when I see you.
Peggy (*emotionally*) Good luck, Doris. I'll be with you all the way.

The Lights fade down

SCENE 2

After a couple of seconds the Lights come up. It is late afternoon

*Doris puts her bag back down again and takes off her coat. She has returned
from court elated*

Doris The prisoner has returned!!
Peggy Doris!
Doris Champagne, Peggy, bugger *Wogan*, I'll do it a bit sloshed. I want to
get so full of fizz, if I uncross my legs I'll shoot out of the window.
Peggy (*anxiously*) So you pulled it off? You got away with it?
Doris "Pulled it off! Got away with it!!" I wasn't flogging a dodgy car,
woman! I was defending my honour and professional integrity. I didn't
"get away" with anything. I wittily, elegantly, and with great restraint shat
on her and rubbed her face in it.
Peggy So I take it you won, then?
Doris Not quite actually won, no, but as good as. They upheld her claim, but
get this, Judgie said he was sick of these big libel awards and that,
personally, he thought that saying a girl had gargantuan love-handles was
a compliment and advised the jury accordingly. She got a tenner damages
and no costs.
Peggy No costs! She'll be completely bankrupt, ruined.
Doris (*mock seriously*) I know, Peggy, and I'm devastated, perhaps you'd
better phone the Samaritans before it all becomes too much for me.

Peggy gets the champagne

Peggy All right, all right, I was only remarking.

Doris A symptom of your celebrated weakness, Peggy, you must toughen up.

Peggy All right, tell me every little mouth-watering detail.

Doris Mouth-watering is exactly the word, Peggy, this case was the legal equivalent of an Opal Fruit. Wait for it, you are simply not going to believe this. They actually measured the silly cow's saddle bags in court.

Peggy No!

Doris Some old bailiff, you know the type, face like a gas bill, had to scurry off for a tape measure… He came back all solemn with a little bag from Woolworth's, "Ninety-two centimetres in trousers, m'lord", he says… I have never seen a woman look a more complete turd in my entire life. I'll tell you what, she's earned her tenner.

Peggy It must have been excrutiating.

Doris We cringed… All except the judge, that is, he's getting all frisky and chipping in that either way a fellow likes something to grab hold of. It was comedy mayhem, believe me.

Peggy Ninety-two centimetres had better not be big; I must be about that or more…

Doris Of course it isn't big, which I suppose is one of the reasons why the silly cow won her case. But the reason she's got nothing out of it is because she's a stupid self-righteous shit and we could all see it. I said it, I said to the judge, I said, "Come off it, Judgie!"

Peggy You didn't!

Doris Well, something like that. I said, "It's bloody obvious that Trudi Hobson is a beautiful woman; she is pert, gorgeous and chewable, with ravishing blonde hair and a lovely figure…" I said, "If a woman like that can't take a good-natured slagging, Gawd help us poor dogs who live in the real world. There are people out there dying of cancer, for God's sake!"

Peggy You don't live in the real world, Doris…

Doris (*enjoying her champagne, draining the glass and refilling it*) Minor point. People think I do. Anyway the judge was lapping it up, wasn't he? Not often for him he gets a dock full of sauce buckets debating the size of their fondle fins. Lucky for me he was a jolly old goat, he was leering away from the start with his wet, watery, yellow eyes, shining like a couple of raw eggs.

Peggy Was she playing up to him?

Doris Was she hell. She was glaring at the floor, I've seen more moving performances in a Renault ad; but I was giving it full cleavage, nothing too obvious, you know, (*she thrusts out her chest*) just that look I've got that says "wrap these round your ears, mate, and I'll breathe on your bald patch".

Peggy Didn't the prosecution say anything?

Doris What could they say? "Objection, m'lud, but will you kindly stop leering at the defendant's coconuts." There are certain things you just don't tell a judge, Peggy. Anyway, then we got into the bit about acting. God you would have loved it... She said she had brought the case on behalf of all those in the public eye who were at the mercy of a new breed of gutter journalism.

Peggy Sounds a bit righteous.

Doris Made me want to carpet the court. I said, "Judgie, this is nothing more than special pleading from a typically self-obsessed actress. So I said she couldn't do her job? There are kids out there taking heroin and nobody gives a damn!!"

Peggy And was this argument judged admissable?

Doris Well, not really, the judge told me to stick to the point but he was nice about it. Luckily for me this woman was her own worst enemy. She called me a brute and a bully. Can you believe it, a bully! It was like something out of a *Girl's Own* annual. A bully. I just said I was entitled to my opinion and that she simply could not act. I was sorry but she was a wooden, lifeless performer with all the genuine histrionic talent of a weatherman and it was my duty to express that fact to the public.

Peggy And what did she say?

Doris She cried, the bitch. I could see the judge going gooey, so I said that crying, m'Lord, is one of the best performances she would ever give; the court loved it.

Peggy Did anyone mention the RSC?

Doris Of course they did, and that was when I clinched it. I mean honestly, Peggy, apart, of course, from the RSC, who gives a toss about the RSC? Ninety per cent of the population never visit the theatre. Nine per cent of the remaining ten have a nice Aberdeen Angus and then go and see *The Milkman's Got My Trousers*, and who goes to the RSC? Eight rows of ponces on the mailing list and fifteen hundred extremely pissed-off school kids.

Peggy I don't know if that argument's really fair, Doris.

Doris Of course it's fair. Anyway, the court must have thought it was fair because, as I say, she won technically but lost in reality, and I, my faithful friend, am off the hook.

Peggy Well, congratulations, Doris, thank God it's over.

Doris Over for me, I don't think it will ever be over for her. I truly believe she's gone completely mad. After we left the courtroom she sort of flipped. She ran up to me and, quite frankly, I've never seen such hatred in anyone. She started to scream at me.

Peggy What did she say?

Doris She said... Oh, it's too bloody stupid, let's forget it.

Evening is falling, the curtains are still open, and very slowly, it is getting darker

Peggy What did she say, Doris?
Doris (*quietly*) She said I was going to die.
Peggy (*concerned*) Not really?
Doris Yes, really. Die publicly. Scorned and humiliated, just as she had done.
Peggy I knew this woman wouldn't be stopped by a judge. She needs help.
Doris (*suddenly screaming*) "Viper! Slut! Filthy cockroach!!!"
Peggy (*shocked*) Please, Doris.
Doris That's what she called me. Right outside the courtroom. Her make-up was all tear-streaked and caked, and she was wearing plenty of it. I have never seen a woman with so much make-up on; she looked like a witch with psoriasis. She threw herself down in front of me and started to tear at her clothes.
Peggy What? In front of everyone?

Peggy has hardly finished her question when Doris hurls herself down before her, grabbing at her

Doris (*screaming again*) "Yes, yes, you're going to die! I swear I'll make you die. You have no human heart, you cannot feel, your soul is the soul of a witch. It is rotten, cold and dead and you must die! You're poison, do you hear me?! Bitter, bitter gall!" And then she turned and ran for a taxi, as if the hounds of hell were after her.
Peggy Poor woman.
Doris Yes, I must confess I felt a twinge. (*After a slightly thoughtful pause, snapping out of it*) Still, sod her, eh? We won! (*She drains her glass*) And tonight we celebrate.

Black-out

ACT II

The same. Immediately following

The Lights come up to find Doris raising her empty glass

Doris Champagne and pizza, that's what we need! Plenty of time before the *Wogan* car comes. Champagne and pizza is the food of the gods and I'm going to stuff it, I'm going to shove it, I'm going to smear pizza all over my body, till I can do an impression of a car crash… *(She grabs the phone and dials)* What do you want on yours, Pegs? I'm having the lot…

Peggy Oh, just a vegetarian please, no peppers, no chilli, no capsicum.

Doris A vegetarian, no peppers, no chilli, no capsicum…! *(Into the phone)* Hallo? Look, I'm afraid I'm going to have to call you back. I appear to be ordering for Mahatma Gandhi. *(She puts the phone down)* Peggy, this is a celebration, you cannot order a dry pizza base.

Peggy I'm not, I want cheese and tomato, it's called a Neapolitan.

Doris A pizza, Peggy, by any other name would be as crap. Calling it a "Neapolitan" means nothing, you could call Little and Large the "Neapolitan" Brothers and they'd still be two Mogadons in velvet bow-ties. This is a party and Neapolitans are not invited.

Peggy All right, I'll have a few mushrooms.

Doris Then let the orgy begin. *(She dials again)* This is the start of a whole new time for me, Peggy, I can feel it. I've dealt with that jumped-up actress, I've got more career options than an ex-cabinet minister, I'm about to order a pizza! I'm in Heaven.

Peggy Beware hubris, Doris.

Doris What's that, something peppery? All right, I'll tell them to hold the hubris.

Peggy It's Greek.

Doris Oh, I love all that stuff, chick-pea, fish roe…

Peggy It's an ancient Greek term. It means pride comes before a fall.

Doris Well, who's a Mrs Hoity Toity… *(Into the phone)* No, not you, I've just got a classically educated killjoy ordering at this end. All right, got your pen ready? I'd like one *(jokingly scornfully)* "Neapolitan", please, with three and a half mushrooms, and two, very large, very deep whoppers, with everything on, yes, that's right everything you've got, the tables, the chairs, the phones, extra hubris. If there is a restaurant cat, slaughter it, put the meat on one and the pelt on the other. Cheesecake, fudge cake, and garlic bread twice. Good, that's the penthouse flat, Morley Mansions. And could you send a slightly less hormonally imbalanced adolescent this time. The last lad who came, I nearly tipped the pizza and ate his face… Ta, gorgeous. (*She puts the phone down*) Now then, Peggy, let's have another glass of that fizz. I feel fantastic.

Peggy It really is good to see you so happy, Doris. You didn't say anything but I knew you were worried about that case.

Doris Well, the woman was so determined, I thought she might sway the judge by just being a mad old witch. That scene outside the court proves she's a lunatic. Yes, there's no question, I'm glad it's over and I can concentrate on the future.

Peggy brings more champagne

Peggy Yes, let's drink to the future.

Doris Up yours, Peggy. It looks pretty bright to me. I'm on a roll, Peggy, everything is opening up for me, and what's more I want you to be a part of it.

Peggy Well, I want to be a part of it, Doris, you know that, but it's not easy.

Doris Now don't be stupid. We've become a team, you and I. Whether I stay in London or go to Stuttgart, you've got to be there.

Peggy Oh, you won't be going to Stuttgart, silly, you know Sid's horrible job is a last option. You'll get the telly.

Doris Well, stranger things have happened.

Peggy I must say I'm a bit concerned about that letter he made you sign though. Supposing you let Sid down and then lost the telly, you'd have to stay where you are. That letter would be a nasty little document to end up on your current editor's desk.

Doris (*happily slightly tiddly*) Peggy, please, I want you to imagine that this small bunch of grapes is our friend Sidney's testicles. (*She snips off the grapes*) Now, were that man to do the dirty on me, I swear, Peggy, I should have his scrotum (*she drops the grapes into the machine*) wrapped round my carriage return and… (*she types the keys very hard*) write his epitaph on them! (*She finishes and viciously slams the carriage return*)

Peggy (*reprovingly*) Well, you're planning to do the dirty on him, Doris.

Doris I am an artist, Peggy, can I help it if I'm being extensively courted?

Peggy You're being extensively deceitful.

Doris That's my prerogative, I'm the one with the talent, let me tell you, Pegs! Once I get a proper shot at telly, all the European Currency Units in Germany wouldn't get me back to print.

Peggy I'm sure they'll take your idea, it's so wonderful, so many shows in one—a talent show, a magazine, a chat show, a weekly review. The title's brilliant.

Doris (*standing exuberantly with her glass*) *A View from the Bitch.*
Peggy I did laugh while I was typing it, when I wasn't trying to decipher your shorthand. Did you really mean *Eurovision* Pong *Contest?*
Doris I most certainly did. It's a Demean the Public section. Guess a bloke's nationality by smelling his breath.
Peggy Oh, I see.
Doris (*rummaging on the table*) So where is this bloody treatment then? I want to make sure you got the Mugging section right.
Peggy Well, it made sense to me. Basically it seems to be a question of taking a handbag from a woman in the audience and showing everybody else what's in it.
Doris You'll never be a poet, Peggy... Oh, look, can you believe it? (*She finds an envelope*) Sidney didn't take his letter after all, drunken old fool.
Peggy I'm sure he did, I saw him take it.
Doris Well he must have put it back, honeyplum, because it's still here and so we remain gloriously uncommitted.
Peggy (*concerned, looking over the table*) Doris, the treatment I typed for you was in an envelope like that...
Doris (*worried*) What? You mean it looked like this? (*She holds up Sidney's letter*)
Peggy I... I think so... (*She realizes*) Oh, my God.
Doris So we've got Sid's letter and he's got my treatment. (*Urgently*) Get Sid on the phone...

Peggy is halfway to the phone when the door intercom buzzer sounds. Peggy and Doris look at each other

It can't be the pizzas, it'll take a month to cook what I ordered...

Peggy crosses to the intercom and answers it

Peggy Hallo? ... Oh, hallo, Mr Skinner. ... Yes, come on up.
Doris Shit.
Peggy He sounded all right.
Doris If he's taken a look in that envelope there's no way he's going to be all right.
Peggy What if he just sent it straight off? I mean, what will the Germans make of it?
Doris Oh, we'll get away with that, I can't see them making much out of the Eurovision Pong Contest. But if he's read it... Oh, well, we shall see, Peggy.

A knock at the door. Peggy opens it

Sidney is outside

Sidney (*cheerfully*) Hallo, Peggy.
Peggy Hallo, Mr Skinner.
Sidney Doris, darling, you won't believe it but your old pal must have had a brain transplant with a house brick. After all that bloody fuss over the letter...
Doris I know, you forgot it. (*She has it in her hand*)
Sidney Gawd, am I thicker than an elephant's sandwich or what? (*He takes it from her*) Thank my stars, thought I might have lost it. (*He takes the paper up stage and, with his back to the audience, puts his briefcase on the sideboard. He opens the case as if to put the paper in; there seems to be a bit of fussing around.* Cheerily*) Well now, Doris, you old jailbird you, tell old Sidney how you got on in court today. I didn't see anything on the news.
Doris (*still not knowing how to play it*) Rather well, actually. I won, basically. Although the silly cow went completely mad afterwards and threatened me with death outside the court.
Sidney Blimey, that's a bit upsetting, I must say.
Doris Oh, don't worry about it, she's harmless enough. All actresses are completely bonkers, they have lobotomies and electric baths at drama school. Ha ha ha!
Sidney No, I mean it's a shame about you winning your case. I don't deny that seeing you dragged off to Holloway in chains would give me greater satisfaction than touching up the gusset on a blurred telephoto shot of Princess Stephanie's crotch.
Doris I beg your pardon.
Sidney You, Doris, are a lying, two-faced slag.
Doris So you read the treatment then?
Sidney Yes, I read it. Congratulations, it was very very good. Rather a complex show to pull off whilst holding a full-time job in Stuttgart, of course, but nonetheless, very, very good.
Doris Thank you.

An embarrassed pause

Peggy (*nervously*) Um, drink, Mr Skinner?
Sidney (*without looking at her*) Fuck off, Peggy.
Doris Um, I'd rather you didn't address my friends like that.
Sidney Oh, friend, is it? I thought she was just some downtrodden little wage slave... (*To Peggy*) I hope you realize, Peggy, that you're probably next under Doris's dancing duvet. Has she started suggesting you wear something prettier yet? Something pink and lacy. Take care, my little virgin prune, this nasty old slut will be under your hem like a greased whippet.

Doris (*suppressing great anger*) And just what is all that supposed to mean, Sidney?

Sidney Come off it, darling one. It's a bit stomach-turning watching a wicked old devil like you trying to play the innocent. Everybody knows about your little preferences, don't they? Except that sad bit of juvenile rough trade, Eduardo, you drag around... He knows now though, I rung him. Cor, those Latin types can't half swear.

Doris Bit pathetic, wasn't it, Sidney? Telling tales to some dirty, stoned kid...

Sidney I'm going to make you regret your lack of standards, Doris.

Doris Oh, for God's sake, all right, I've been investigating other work. So what? It probably won't come off, and then you and I will be spitting blood at each other in Stuttgart as if nothing had happened.

Sidney I'm not going to Stuttgart. I've already faxed them, I've blown it out.

Doris Sidney, you're raving. You reckon that because I've been a bit of a naughty girl, you're going to make yourself redundant?

Sidney I'm not going to be redundant, darling. At least I hope not. If negotiations that I put in train this afternoon come off, I'm going to be fronting an outrageous new talent, magazine, chat show on Sky TV.

Doris (*very heavily*) What are you talking about, Sidney?

Sidney Oh, I know it seems unlikely, dear. An old tart like me becoming a star, but I have got a certain common touch, don't you think? And anyway, the ideas I had to offer, well, the producer had a bloody orgasm. I must say, I thought he'd be pleased, ideas were rather good you see... the "Pong" contest, the handbag bit, great for a man to do it too.

Doris starts forward. Sidney grabs a bottle

Don't you bloody hit me, you gorilla-faced dyke!

Doris I'll sue you for plagiarism...!!

Sidney Oh, yeah? Who have you got? You and your mousy little girlfriend here? Don't make me damp my jocks. I'll get a witness too, I'll get ten. Copyright is about proving first ownership, my gorgeous old sauce. My idea's with a producer at Sky, who's seen yours?

Doris Sid, you pig, if you pull this off, which you won't let me tell you, I shall crucify you every week in print for ever. What I did to that silly cow in court today will look like a character reference from Postman Pat.

Sidney Not in your present rag it won't, my dear. You see, as I believe I mentioned earlier, this case has a portable fax machine in it, Cellnet you see, very clever. (*He takes the letter of intent out again*) I didn't think that your current editor would take kindly to you signing a letter of intent to German publishers, so I've sent him a copy.

Doris You ... didn't!

Sidney I did, my love. Faxed it through to him just now. If the lazy sod's still at work, he'll have it by now... (*He walks to the door*) So there you go, Doris, Europe's out, you've almost certainly lost your present job, and I've nicked your game show. That is what you get for being a dirty double-crosser.

Sid exits

Doris rushes to the door and shouts after him

Doris You're dead, do you hear me, Sid, dead!

Peggy I'm so sorry, Doris...

Doris I can't believe it, the bastard, I've got to think... Why did you make me drink that bloody champagne, Peggy? I've got to think... I need something to help me think... (*She crosses to the sideboard. She is looking for something. She searches for a moment*) Peggy, I've told you never to clear anything up, or throw anything away from here.

Peggy I haven't... What...?

Doris An envelope that Eduardo brought round... There was an envelope here when I left for court!!

Peggy An empty envelope, yes...

Doris It wasn't bloody empty! It had a little package in the bottom of it, an important little package.

Peggy A package of what?

Doris Never mind what, where's the bloody envelope?

Peggy I... I ... used it.

Doris Peggy, what do you mean?

Peggy I always re-use old envelopes... I've got these re-sealing stickers from Friends of the Earth... It was empty, I...

Doris (*shouting*) It wasn't bloody empty!!

Peggy (*very upset*) Please, Doris, don't shout, I don't understand. What was in it?

Doris Never mind what was in it, who did you send it to?

Peggy It was your VAT tax forms from Douglas.

Doris (*exploding in disbelief*) The Customs and Excise!! You sent eight grams of cocaine to Her Majesty's Customs and Excise!!

Peggy Cocaine? Doris, I had no idea you...

Doris Where's my passport? I've got to pack! Peggy, phone the travel agent, I have to get out. Oh, my God! I've got to pack. This can't be happening!

Peggy I didn't send it to Customs, I sent it to Douglas.

Doris Douglas?

Peggy That was what I was supposed to do, wasn't it?

Doris (*stopping*) Douglas? That's better ... probably wouldn't even know what it was, don't think he'd shop me... Peggy, get him on the phone...

Peggy grabs the phone

Look at these, Peggy… (*She goes to her desk, starts grabbing handfuls of envelopes*) Envelopes, envelopes, we are surrounded by hundreds of bloody envelopes… Peggy, the trees are already dead, I don't think they would have minded… Oh, God, why me!

Sidney appears at the door again, with Eduardo

Sidney Knock, knock. Excuse I. Just wait and see who I've found, trying to kick the door down; he's bust your outside lock… Thought I'd bring him up, wouldn't want to miss the fun.

He leans arrogantly against the door as Eduardo pushes past him

Peggy (*to Doris*) Douglas is out. (*She puts the phone down, crosses to the door*) Eduardo, this isn't a good time.

Eduardo is furious—seething with injured pride. He looks ready for violence

Eduardo Oh, yeah, Pegs doll? I reckon it's a raving good time. Awesome. Anybody want a couple of lines of Gonzales? It's top gear, banging good stuff. "Columbian". Got it off a Rasta. Totally wasted my box. Murder, man.

Doris Get out, Eduardo. I'll phone you.

Eduardo You can stick your phone up your brown-eyed cyclops, you horrible old tart.

Doris What?

Eduardo (*shouting*) Why didn't you tell me you was a muff muncher?

Doris Listen, sonny, I'll tell you exactly what I like and when I like, and what I'm telling you now is to fuck off and take your foul, fucking mouth with you.

Eduardo (*beginning to let his anger show*) Listen, Babes, I don't mind being pampered but I ain't being used, all right? I got standards. I'll take 'em fat, I'll take 'em ugly, but I don't take them queer. You made a fool of me. You … you made me look dirty in front of the geezers.

Doris Excuse me, but this is now becoming just a touch comical. I've had a tabloid editor talking about privacy, now I've got a rather inexpensive toy boy saying he feels soiled. Well, you are soiled, Eduardo, that's how you were born. Brillo pads and Liquid Gumption couldn't raise the ghost of a shine on you.

Eduardo leaps forward and grabs her

Eduardo Yeah, and you're a dirty pervert! Your sort should get put away! Bloody corrupt kids you do!

Peggy You leave her alone you ... peanut prick!

Eduardo turns on Peggy

Eduardo What's shakin' now, eh? What's cooking, Pegs? Raving got you, ain't I? Raving got you, you old dog. (*He raises his fist to strike*)

Peggy Hit a woman would you, you coward!

Eduardo Why not? I ain't Saint raving George, am I? Besides, your kind ain't women. Bet you molest kids, it's always in the papers that stuff is. Makes me want to have a right classic spew.

Doris Peggy, phone the police, tell them we have two dangerous intruders...

Eduardo calms quickly

Eduardo No need for all that.

Sidney Oh, don't trouble yourself on my behalf, I shall be off shortly. Just finishing my drink and watching the fun...

Doris All right, Peggy.

Eduardo (*triumphantly*) You want to know something, Doris! You thought you kept your little secret pretty good, didn't yah? Well, I've blown it, yeah, classic giggle. Stitched you up proper, you slag. Want to know what I did? I told the papers. Awesome, eh? I told them about us and what you really are...

Sidney "Teenage toy boy denounces middle-aged celebrity girlfriend as gay".

Doris I am not middle-aged!

Eduardo goes to the door

Eduardo So see you, doll, gonna have a decent rage for once, ain't I? Do some blow, get on some "E". Hang out with some happening people, people who ain't half dead. You won't see me again. Except one thing, babe, we'll be together one more time, in the Sunday papers, ha ha ha! Awesome, eh?

Sidney Thank you for the drink, Doris... Actually, you won't believe this, but I'm sorry. You're having a slightly more rotten evening than even I had planned.

Doris You've got five seconds.

Sidney OK. Just trying to be nice.

Sidney pauses for a second, then exits

Long pause

Peggy (*pretty shaken*) What ... what are we going to do, Doris?
Doris Something very strange is going on, Peggy, too much is happening at once.

Douglas appears at the door. He is stern and angry. He is holding the envelope

Douglas The outside door lock has been forced, I presume by those two hooligans I just passed on the stairs. Anyway, I took the liberty of coming up.

Peggy and Doris jump

Doris Hallo, Douglas.
Douglas (*sternly*) Good evening, Miss Wallis.
Doris (*nervously correcting him*) Doris, Douglas.
Douglas I think under the circumstances I would prefer a less familiar form of greeting.
Doris Circumstances, Douglas?
Douglas I was with the Customs and Excise for fifteen years, I know the hellish stuff when I see it.
Doris Well, don't cry about it, for God's sake. It's only for private, recreational...
Douglas Oh, private is it? Damn strange kind of privacy, popping it in with your VAT returns and sending it to your accountant. It's the breathless arrogance of your kind that makes me so very angry. Why do you consider yourself so different, Miss Wallis? Why is it that people like you, fashionable people, can indulge yourselves in any kind of unhealthy, anti-social activity that you choose and continue to lead comfortable, respectable lives, while half the civilized world watches its children die over stuff like this... (*He shakes the envelope at her*)
Doris Look, Douglas, I'm having a particularly tough day today and I'm not sure I'm up to a moral debate.
Douglas No! No, I don't think you are up to a moral debate, you nasty, hypocritical woman.
Doris Douglas, I'm sorry the stuff has offended you so much, I really am, and I'll think about what you've said ... but, for now, why don't you give it me back and then you can forget all about it, eh?
Douglas (*very angry*) Do you know there are Asian women doing fifteen years in Holloway for getting this stuff to you? Poor, clueless mules. I know, I caught a few, and a bloody depressing business it was too. Fishing

small, damp packages out of people's bottoms made me feel like a bloody magician.

Doris Yes, well, I'm very sorry for them...

Douglas Good! Good! I'm glad you're sorry for them, it's nice that you're sorry for them, because you're shortly going to have the pleasure of being able to tell them so yourself.

Peggy (*stunned*) Douglas, no!

Doris What the hell are you talking about, Douglas?

Douglas Oh, come now, Miss Wallis, you know me well enough to realize that I am not and never have been one of these types, so common in the last decade, who believe that they need only obey those parts of the law which they choose. Oh, well, I know you think me a senile old fool.

Doris Yes.

Douglas It doesn't matter anyway, I just wanted you to understand my point of view. It's a police matter now. (*He turns to go to the door*)

Doris You'd better stop right there, Douglas! (*She grabs a paper knife*)

Douglas is at the door

Douglas How very fitting, how very apt. My entire thesis is confirmed, out comes the flick-knife, the switch-blade.

Doris Douglas, it's a paper knife.

Douglas Rich or poor, this is where drugs will inevitably lead you. It will be gang colours, automatic assault rifles and shoulder-held missile launchers next. Goodbye, Miss Wallis. I am sorry for you.

Doris Grab him, Peggy. (*She drops the knife, leaps at him and grabs him*)

But Douglas spins her round and pins her to the wall. During the following, Peggy discreetly gets something out of her handbag

Douglas Don't be a fool, madam! I was eight years a soldier...

Doris Peggy!!

Peggy coshes Douglas, who falls to the ground, senseless, by the sofa

Peggy Oh, my God!

Doris Oh, my God. (*Approvingly*) Nice move, Peggy. I had no idea you carried a cosh. (*She grabs the envelope, checks it*)

Peggy My mother makes me.

Doris And quite right too. Thank you very much, Douglas, and, incidently, when you wake up you're sacked.

Peggy (*kneeling beside Douglas, stunned*) He's dead.

Doris He can't be.

Peggy (*very upset*) He is.

Doris The bastard.

Peggy (*suddenly she screams hysterically*) Ahhhhh! What have I done, what have I done? I've killed him! Why didn't you tell me you took drugs, why didn't you say?

Doris Come on, Peggy! Calm down, love, calm down. We're in this together, we'll work it out. (*She hugs her*) We've got plenty of time, we'll make a plan. Yes, that's it, we'll make a plan. Nobody knows about this, nobody's coming to get you… Nobody's coming to get you.

The door intercom buzzer sounds. They both jump mightily. Both scream

Peggy Save me, Doris, you've got to save me, I don't want to go to prison…

Doris Nobody's going to prison, stay calm, stay calm. (*She crosses to the intercom, gingerly answers it*) Hallo… (*To Peggy*) It's the pizzas. (*Into the intercom*) I love you, but we don't really want them any more, we… Oh, all right, the front door's broken, come on up. (*To Peggy*) Can you believe it, he wants his money…

Peggy But … but … if he comes in here, he'll see…

Doris Don't be stupid, he's not coming in here, is he? You've got to calm down, take this money and meet him at the stairs and pay him…

Peggy Well… No, I can't.

Doris You've got to, everything must be as normal as possible. Now we're going to get through this together, Peggy. So take some money, go outside and pay the pizza man … and don't mention the corpse.

Peggy Right.

Peggy reluctantly takes her handbag and goes out

Doris takes the envelope and hides the drugs under the typewriter. Suddenly all the Lights go out. Doris screams in shock in the darkness. She lights a lighter and finds her way across to the candelabras on the sideboard. She begins to light them

Peggy appears at the door, laden with pizzas

Doris (*peering*) Is that you, Peggy?

Peggy (*with a shaky voice*) Yes, it's me … the lights have gone out.

Doris I know that, Peggy.

Peggy It must be a main fuse, the whole building seems to have gone, the emergency lights are on in the stairwell.

Doris Well, it's nice to know that some misfortunes are not exclusive to me.

She has all the candles going, the light is dim and flickering

Peggy (*laden with enormous pizza boxes*) I've got the pizzas.

Doris I'm not really hungry anymore. We have to do something with this body.

Peggy (*weeping on her shoulder*) How… there's people in the street, on the stairs, we'll be caught, I know we'll be caught.

Doris Well, if we can't get it out, we've got to give it a good reason to be here…

Peggy (*trying to think*) Well … well … he came to check something about your accounts.

Doris Yes, not bad as far as it goes, but it doesn't explain why he's dead, does it?

Peggy It's my fault, Doris, I killed him, I should take the consequences. What … what if I cosh you as well, to prove you weren't involved, then call the police and tell them I went mad?

Doris I don't know if you noticed, Peggy, but the last time you coshed someone they ended up dead.

Peggy Well, I could be gentle.

Doris No, I don't want you to.

Peggy Well, what if I tied you up?

Doris Yes, good thinking, Peggy, not bad, but it's got to look like he was the aggressor. Yes, that's good actually, Peg. Now come on, tie me up, we'll do it here.

Peggy Have you got any rope?

Doris Yes, loads in the bedroom.

Peggy Good. Why?

Doris Never mind about that now… I'm scared of fires, it's for escaping, now go and get it. It's in the wardrobe, Peggy, and there's a set of handcuffs under the pillow, bring those as well.

Peggy Right.

Peggy goes into the bedroom

Doris sits in the chair up stage, facing the audience

Peggy returns with rope and handcuffs

Doris Now, we've got to get the plot straight. These are the basics, Peggy, OK? We plant the coke on his corpse so that we can say he came round to blackmail me, and in the process ties me up.

Peggy But, Doris, none of these things happened.

Doris I know that, Peggy, but he's not here to deny it, is he? Now tie me up!

Peggy reluctantly begins to do it

Peggy I still don't see...
Doris God, you're so thick sometimes, Peggy. Listen, he's tied me up, right?
He's threatening me with blackmail, OK? You return, having popped out
for some hubris to put on the pizzas ... there's a struggle, during which you
triumph, all right? It's just our word, there's nobody else to tell a different
story, we'll get away with it. Tighter, Peggy, it has to be convincing.
Peggy (*struggling*) I'm doing my best, Doris...
Doris Ow! Yes, that's tight enough, I can't move.
Peggy There, that's pretty good, I was a Girl Guide, you know.
Doris Fascinating; handcuffs. Now get the coke from under the typewriter,
I hid it there. Put it in his pocket and then you can ring the police...

Peggy gets the envelope. She returns to Doris

Peggy I'm scared, Doris.
Doris (*gently*) Don't be scared, Peggy, I'll look after you. Really, Peggy, I
mean it. I'll always protect you. Now just put the package in Douglas's
pocket...

Peggy puts it in Doris's pocket

No, Douglas's pocket, Peggy, watch my lips, darling. Put the drugs in
Douglas's pocket...

Peggy is still tightening the ropes

Put the drugs in Douglas's pocket.
Peggy (*gently, but straight into Doris's face*) So, I can't act, can I?
Doris What?
Peggy So you don't think I can act.

*Doris screams suddenly. In the flickering half-light Peggy tears off her
brunette wig; underneath she is blonde*

(*Shouting in Doris's face*) Viper! Slut! Filthy cockroach!! You have no
human heart, you cannot feel, your soul is the soul of a witch. It is rotten,
cold and dead and you must die! You're poison, do you hear me?! Bitter,
bitter gall!

*Peggy is Trudi Hobson; she now becomes her, turning before our eyes into
an eccentrically mannered actress. Her walk changes into the slightly showy
elegance of those who value their dance training, no matter how many years
ago it was. Her accent becomes the casual but terribly refined drawl of those
who have been taught how to speak properly. She pushes her wild blonde hair*

*off her forehead. The quiet, mousy Peggy has completely vanished. Although
she will continue to be called that*

Yes, darling. It's me. The silly cow you said couldn't act. Well, I've acted
pretty well the last six months, haven't I, darling? (*She walks to the door*)
I'll just make us more cosy, shall I? Wouldn't want to be disturbed, would
we? Now, I can pop the fusette back in so you can take a really good look
at who I am.

She steps outside for a moment

The Lights come back on

Doris This isn't possible.

Peggy enters

Peggy That's theatre, love. The art of the not-possible, a wonderful world of
make-believe which we, the actors, make you believe in. Oh, it's easier
than you think when one puts one's mind to it. A good cossie and wig,
impeccable references forged by a sweet, sweet prop master I know. I
offered maximum enthusiasm for minimum salary and you fell for it.

Doris But it's … it's so totally out of proportion.

Peggy Out of proportion? Darling, you ain't seen nothing yet. The play isn't
over.

Doris What are you going to do?

Peggy Destroy you, my dear. I swore from the very first moment, win or lose,
I would bring you down. Oh, it hasn't been so very arduous. Seven hours
acting, three days a week. At Rose Bru' we thought nothing of improvising
through the night; all we needed was a bottle of cheap plonk, a fragment
of Strindberg and we were in Heaven.

Doris You're mad, totally raving barking out of your ruddy tree!

Peggy (*pouring herself a drink*) Well, do you know, I think all actors have
to be a little mad, or how could we do what we do? We're so very different
from ordinary people, you see. We hurt so very deeply. That is why I had
to plan my wicked plan, do you see? I had to do it. The actress in me said
I must. And, oh, what a performance! The most wonderful and fulfilling
of my career.

Doris There is a dead accountant on the carpet!

Peggy Yes, that's a bonus I must say.

Doris Peggy…

Peggy Trudi, darling. Peggy is a character, a part; I loathe these young actors
who can't distance themselves from their characters, don't you? It's so
silly.

Doris Trudi...

Peggy All that method rubbish about "becoming" someone, well it's just Americanized bollocks, darling, it really is, absolute Yank wank. An actor acts, for heaven's sake, it's a job of work and a bloody hard one too.

Doris Six months, Trudi, six months you've kept up this bit of "acting".

Peggy Well, you paid me, and, besides, I was resting anyway. Oh, there was a bit of telly around, but nothing happening in the West End at all. The place is a morgue.

Doris Six months, I mean, why, for God's sake?

Peggy Oh, I know it was naughty and I shouldn't have done it, darling; we in the business are always taught to develop a thick skin where the reviews are concerned... How, I ask? It's absurd—ask an actor to develop a thick skin? You might as well ask a flower to develop iron petals...

Doris But it was just a comment, Trudi, a bit of newsprint...

Peggy It damn well hurt. I mean, obviously one knows that all reviews except the sweet ones are maddeningly silly drivel, the ravings of a lunatic, and what's more, a lunatic who simply has not taken the trouble to understand the piece ... but you are not even a critic, you wicked woman, you and your kind are no more than mindless bullies. Can't act!! Can't act, by God! I've destroyed your life by acting. I've acted you to the ground. It was I who switched papers on that repulsive man Skinner so that he took away your equally repulsive show treatment...

Doris Yes, all right, very clever but...

Peggy It was I who informed him of your queenly sexuality, in the hope that he might use it against you.

Doris (*getting angry*) Listen, you mad bitch...!

Peggy It was I who quite deliberately used your envelope full of drugs to send off your accounts.

Doris It was you who killed a man, Trudi! He's lying there in front of the sofa and forgive me but I don't notice him applauding your performance.

Peggy I didn't kill him.

Doris Yes, you did, you coshed the silly old git and he died.

Peggy Oh, don't be absurd. What would Trudi Hobson the actress be doing in the flat of her arch enemy, murdering people? I've never been here, I don't even know where it is...

Doris Now come on, Peggy...

Peggy Exactly, Peggy! Who's Peggy? A shadow, a figment, nothing more than a performance. Without me she's gone. And I won't be here. So perhaps it was you that killed Douglas...

Doris I didn't kill him and you know it. Peggy killed him.

Peggy I say again, who's Peggy? She's fading fast... Did I play her? It seems so strange, after all (*into Doris's face*) I can't act, can I?

Doris Listen, Trudi Hobson, you are obviously deeply and irredeemably mad, but please, for me, make an effort, clutch for a final moment at the coat tails of Mrs Sanity as she scuttles from your mind forever, and understand that I will not be taking your rap.

Peggy But, my dear, I really don't see how you can avoid it. Because when the police get involved, as eventually they must, there will only be you and the corpse left on my little stage.

Doris Whenever the police get involved I'll still be tied up, or perhaps he tied me up after he got killed?

Peggy begins to collect her things

Peggy You won't be tied up, I wasn't that good a Girl Guide. You'll worm yourself free eventually, you'll have to. Your answerphone is on and Peggy's last act was to cancel your appointments. You'll either untie yourself or starve. And when you are free again, you'll be all alone with the corpse and the cocaine and it will be your turn to create a convincing performance.

Doris Sid, Eduardo, they know Peggy existed. They'll say Peggy was real.

Peggy is putting the wig back on—preparing to depart

Peggy I really can't see either of those two low-lifes getting involved in a murder enquiry on your behalf. And as to the others I've dealt with, I've been careful to do your business strictly by phone. There are very few people who have caught so much as a glimpse of shy, retiring Peggy. Still, you can ring them when you get yourself free, if you can find your phone book, which I doubt, after all, as you've often said in the last month or two, without Peggy you wouldn't know where your arse was to wipe it. Which, since Peggy is a figment of my imagination, doesn't say much for you, you nasty, pig-ignorant bully.

Sidney appears at the door

Sidney Someone mention my name?
Doris (*with enormous relief*) Sidney, thank God you're here.

Sidney hovers at the door

Sidney Well, it's very nice of you to say so, Doris, I had no idea we were still friends. Just come back for my fax machine—always forgetting it.
Doris No, Sid, look, she's tied me up.

Sidney advances into the room

Sidney Well, there seems to be something of an orgy going on here.
Doris Sid, you don't understand.

Sidney Oh, I think I do, Doris—don't mind me, I'm broad minded, I've
travelled. No chance of a "ménage", I suppose?
Doris Sidney, listen to me. Peggy's not Peggy… She's that actress, she's
killed Douglas. Look, he's dead.

Sidney sees the corpse which had been shielded from him by the sofa

Sidney Bugger my bollocks!
Peggy She's gone mad, Mr Skinner. She killed Mr Robertson. I had to tie her
up to restrain her. Now, I'm just going for the police, so will you please let
me pass?
Doris Don't let her go, Sydney. Look at her hair, it's a wig.

Sidney peers at Peggy

Peggy Don't you dare touch me, Mr Skinner. Don't you dare.

He reaches out and plucks off her wig

Sidney It's Trudi bloody Hobson.
Peggy Yes, it's Trudi bloody Hobson. I fooled you just as I fooled that literary
pigmy over there. Even though, apparently, I can't act.
Doris Oh, shut your face, you stupid mad cow. Sidney, you've got to restrain
that woman, she's gone totally berserk.
Sidney Why should I?
Doris What do you mean, why? So we can phone the police and have her
locked up in the looney bin for criminally insane actors…
Peggy Please, don't send me to the National!
Doris What are you hanging around for, Sidney. Tie her up or something.
Sidney No.
Doris What?
Sidney I'm not going to help you.
Doris Sidney, please.
Sidney I'm going to let Peggy's little plan take its predetermined course, as
if I'd never come back for my fax machine. (*He gives Peggy back her wig*)
No point messing with a good script, is there? Can't go changing the ending
just because some old arse like me blunders in from the wings. No, on the
whole, I think I shall leave you two witches dancing around your cauldron.
Doris (*desperately*) Sidney, please help me. You've got to help me!
Sidney I'm afraid old Sid the pig can't help you, my saucy darling… After
all, who's Sidney?
Doris What?
Sidney (*walking up to her and straight in her face*) So I can't act, can I?
Doris Oh, my fucking God.

Sidney now drops his Sid yobbo character. He is an actor, a tough, northern one, Liverpool Everyman or Glasgow Citizen type of thing, strong regional accent. Plenty of leftish, earthy posing, but every bit the "actor" that Peggy is

Sidney I was bloody superb in that Alan Bleasdale series, but obviously a Tory cow like you working for a Tory rag was never ever remotely going to even try to understand the piece. That wasn't genuine criticism, that was political propaganda.

Doris tries to speak, but is too gobsmacked

Peggy You were, Tom, you were quite superb.
Sidney Of course I was. When I played that Bleasdale brickie on BBC 2, I suffered more than any real brickie has ever suffered, I worked harder than any brickie has ever worked! I was every brickie.
Peggy So in many ways you worked as hard and suffered as much as all the brickies in the world put together.
Sidney Well, I think that's what Alan wanted.
Peggy Marvellous text.
Sidney (*turning back to Doris*) So there's me taking the collective suffering of the entire building trade on my shoulders, without claiming my full Equity tea-break entitlement, I might add.
Peggy God, you're a trooper.
Sidney And what did you have to say? I got my flipping accent wrong! You stupid cow! His accent was supposed to be wrong! That was the whole point, the poor bastard didn't know who he was! That was what I was trying to say, I mean I really wouldn't have minded if you'd taken the trouble to understand the piece.
Doris (*still a bit stunned*) So you've been working with each other from the start.
Peggy It's my production, I sought Tom out... You were marvellous, darling, truly incandescent.
Sidney Aye, well it's worked out bloody well, hasn't it? (*He kicks Douglas*) The death was a bonus though, that'll really stitch the cow.
Peggy Well, exactly. But you really were marvellous.
Sidney No, no, you were, much tougher role. I could just go for laughs, you had to carry the emotion, the content.
Doris And so what's next for the Bonkers Twins then? Two ends of a pantomime Napoleon in *Looney Bin, the Musical*?
Peggy My dear woman, as I have explained, we are actors, we are supposed to be a little mad. And now, sadly, it is goodbye, Miss Wallis, I do hope you enjoyed our performance.
Doris No.
Sidney I was on that building site for an entire morning—I knew those men.

They are leaving

Doris Stop, please. Come back.
Peggy Well, darling.
Sidney I suppose we must.

They walk back into the room

Doris Good. Right, let's just talk about this as adults, what is it you want from me … money?

They bow

(*Calling out*) What! What are you doing? You can't do this to me!!

They bow again

Sidney (*to Peggy*) One more, love?
Peggy No, I think we'd be milking it. Drinky time I think.

Sidney and Peggy leave

There is a long pause

Doris (*struggling*) Come back!! Come back, you mad actors… (*She struggles again*) Come back… (*With more struggling, she screams dramatically at the top of her voice*) All right, I admit it, you can act, you can act, you can act!!

Douglas raises his head from the floor and speaks in a huge actor's voice

Douglas Act. And what about me, you horrid woman!

Doris shrieks. Douglas leaps up. He is now not Douglas at all, but an actor of the old school, a deep velvet-voiced luvvie, who never got to play Lear, a mad, outrageous old ham

(*With a huge voice*) "Blow winds and crack your cheeks!" (*With a tiny voice*) "Tell me not now that Little Nell is dead"… (*He walks over and stands over her*) Isn't that acting, madam! Have I not the muse!
Doris I want my mum.
Douglas (*a huge performance*) Just so have I, a thousand times, yearned for the comfort of a mother's breast, when I recall your cruel jibe, "Dickhead of the Day". Twice in the *Preston Clarion* did you give me such a title!

"Ham", you called me! Ham! I, madam, am an actor! I know of no such
meat. Noël Coward impressions, I knew the master quite well actually and
he would have laughed at the suggestion.
Doris So you're not dead then?
Douglas No, foul woman, I am not dead. I live to taste the sweet knowledge
that you thought I was dead, just as you thought I was your accountant,
whom Peggy so conveniently found for you. You thought both these
things, foul lady, even though, apparently, (*into her face*) I cannot act...

Eduardo appears at the door

Eduardo Happening, what's shakin' slag?
Doris Oh, Christ.
Eduardo (*walking in*) Thought this geezer was your accountant, now he's
tying you up. (*To Douglas*) You giving her a portion or what? (*To Doris*)
He your toy grandad then? Happening. Anyway, if you two are up for a bit
of rumpy-pumpy, I won't keep you, just wanted some dosh for that toot I
scored you, I forgot before...
Doris Come off it, Eduardo, get it over with, pull your nose off and show me
who you are... Felicity Kendal?
Eduardo Oh, this is classic, what have you been puffing, Doris? I wish I'd
had some, it must be banging good gear, eh, Dougy boy?
Douglas I answer to no such name, young man.
Eduardo Eh? You been blowing and all, have you?
Doris Eduardo, don't tell me you're a real person, you're not an actor!

*Eduardo glares at Doris. Suddenly he drops the wide-boy act and becomes
what he is, a beautiful, sensitive, pretentious, young actor*

Eduardo Actors are real people, you bitch. Just because we're talented and
special doesn't mean we don't bleed. People still call me "that poof off the
ravioli ads", because of you. I was making fifty thousand pounds a year
when they dropped me. I had to give up my clowning, my mime classes.
I am a half-trained mime! Can you imagine the emptiness? I know how to
get into the glass box but I can't get out of it.
Douglas Poor boy. How you young lions torment yourselves.
Eduardo Yes, thanks, mate.
Doris This isn't happening.

Peggy and Sidney enter

Peggy I see that you two loves have both had your *coup de théâtre*'s then?
Douglas And sweet it was, my dear lady, sweet it was.

Eduardo (*anguished*) I wasn't happy with mine, it was a disaster... It wasn't centred, it wasn't consistent...

Douglas But, my boy, you were wonderful, wonderful.

Eduardo No, I wasn't. I was crap. I know I was crap, oh, God, I don't know why I even kid myself that I can act. It's a joke, a ruddy joke, me an actor?

Peggy Oh, darling!

Eduardo Ha! I know I'm better than any other actor of my generation, but what the hell does that prove?

Douglas Poor, dear boy, tearing yourself apart inside. You'll learn, young fellow, you'll learn. Suffering is part of your apprenticeship... (*To Sidney*) I enjoyed you, Tom, that was a wicked improvisation though, kicking me while I was down—I nearly grunted.

Sidney Oh, I knew you were too much the pro for that, mate.

Douglas Ah, yes, playing a corpse is a tough job of acting. So many young fellows think you just have to be physically still. Wrong! You have to be brain dead.

Sidney Anyway, pays you back for putting that tampon in the handbag when we were doing *The Importance* at Hull, do you remember?

Douglas (*laughing*) God, that's a good story, that one. The tampon in the handbag in Hull. I don't think Trudi's heard that one.

Peggy Do you know, I don't believe I have.

Doris Oh, God!

Sidney Well, me and this hell-raising old sod were playing *The Importance* at Hull, freezing cold winter, no heating in the dressing rooms. And then one night his nibs here decides to raise a little Hades. Well, my liege only goes and puts a tampon in the handbag, doesn't he!?

Peggy shrieks

Douglas God, we raised some hell though, didn't we?

Sidney Aye, we supped some decent pints.

Peggy A tampon, priceless.

Eduardo When I'm on stage, I'm dying inside.

Sidney And so you should be at your age. You can raise some hell when you've learnt your flipping craft and not before. If you're looking for an easy life in the theatre, become a bloody agent.

Peggy Oh, don't, mine's a nightmare—ten per cent for bugger all.

They are all about to tell their agent stories

Doris Excuse me, I don't want to keep you, I know you're all anxious to get your strait-jackets fitted but do you mind if I clear up one or two points here?

Peggy Of course, an actor must always encourage audience feedback.

Eduardo (*squatting down*) Perhaps we should workshop it?

Douglas I fear you must count me out if you do, dear boy. I would look an absolute sight in a leotard.

Doris I just want to get the plot straight... There never was a Euro job?

Peggy Of course not.

Doris And nobody has stolen my idea for Sky, or told the press about my girlfriends, or faxed Sidney's letter to my boss?

Sidney Props love, ever heard of 'em? The actor is given an empty case, the audience perceive a portable fax machine. That is what makes actors special.

Douglas Hear, hear.

Eduardo Hey, Tom. I think it would have been really good if you'd mimed the case. What do you think, mate?

Sidney Somehow I don't think she would have bought that, son.

Doris (*cutting in*) And no-one's told the police about my little habits, or anything...

Peggy Nothing has happened, darling, nothing at all. It was a play, don't you see, you've just been in a play.

Sidney And now the play is nearly over.

Douglas Drinky time.

Peggy Hear, hear.

Eduardo I might join you if there's time, but I like to unwind, alone, for a moment or two after the catharsis.

Sidney Well, yes, a couple of years carrying a spear in laddered tights will knock that out of you, son. But now our audience must applaud us... (*He gestures at Doris*)

Peggy, Douglas and Eduardo exit

Doris What?

Sidney Oh, yes, the most important part is yet to come. You, Doris Wallis, and you alone, must applaud us all. We must hear your ringing approbation, your heartfelt tribute to actors who, in your humble, ignorant opinion, can act... Can you do it?

Doris (*woodenly*) Yes.

Sidney Go on, have a little practice, we don't want to spoil the final moment...

Doris claps

Oh, come on, I think we deserve more than that.

Doris claps louder

Right, keep it going… And so ladies and … well, lady anyway, it's a small
audience, but it's not the size of your audience, it's the size of your
performance. So would you, Doris Wallis, please welcome back into your
sitting-room Quentin Hopkins who played the part of Eduardo the toy
boy…

*Eduardo enters and takes a bow (with his back to the audience) as Doris
applauds*

I think one or two "bravos" might be in order, eh?
Doris *(woodenly)* Bravo.
Sidney All right, son, don't milk it. Kelvin Cruikshank as Douglas
Robertson the accountant…

Douglas enters and bows

Doris *(clapping)* Bravo.
Sidney And myself, Tom Warwick, Sid the editor… *(he bows and raises a
fist)* fight the cuts.
Doris Bravo, *(after a pause)* you wanker.
Sidney And finally, you will be applauding our leading lady, who for the
remainder of the evening will be taking over the part of Doris Wallis!!

*Peggy enters. She is dressed exactly as Doris, her hair and make-up are
the same, she looks just like her*

Doris stops clapping

Doris What?
Sidney Oh, yes, she said you were going to die, Doris, die the public
humiliation that she did. And you will, pal, you will … tonight your public
will watch you die.

The door intercom buzzer sounds. Eduardo answers it

Eduardo *(into the intercom)* Hallo… *(To Peggy)* It's the car for *Wogan.*
Peggy Tell them I'll be right down.

Black-out

THE END

FURNITURE AND PROPERTY LIST

Further dressing may be added at the director's discretion

ACT I

SCENE 1

On stage: Sofa
    Sideboard. *On it:* bottles of drink including champagne, glasses,
      2 candelabras. Bowl containing fruit, including grapes
    Desk. *On it:* envelopes, papers, pen, paper knife, typewriter, phone
    Chair
    Intercom
    Mirror
    TV
    Court bag
    Doris's coat
    Doris's scarf

Off stage: Ancient leather briefcase containing papers (**Douglas**)
    Bunch of flowers (**Eduardo**)
    Briefcase containing newspaper cutting, bag (**Peggy**)

Personal: **Douglas:** coat
    Eduardo: watch, envelope
    Peggy: watch

SCENE 2

On stage: As before

ACT II

On stage: As before

Off stage: Briefcase (**Sidney**)
                Envelope (**Douglas**)
                Pizza boxes (**Peggy**)
                Rope and handcuffs (**Peggy**)

LIGHTING PLOT

Property fittings required: nil
1 interior setting. The same throughout

ACT I, SCENE 1

To open: Overall general lighting

Cue 1   **Peggy**: "I'll be with you all the way."   (Page 18)
               Fade lights down

ACT I, SCENE 2

To open: Late afternoon lighting

Cue 2   **Doris**: "Oh, it's too bloody stupid, let's forget it."   (Page 20)
               Begin to fade slowly to evening lighting

Cue 3   **Doris**: "And tonight we celebrate."   (Page 21)
               Black-out

ACT II

To open: Overall general lighting

Cue 4   **Doris** hides the drugs under the typewriter   (Page 32)
               Black-out

Cue 5   **Doris** lights the candles   (Page 32)
               Flicker effect of candles

Cue 6   After **Peggy** steps outside   (Page 35)
               Bring up lights

Cue 7   **Peggy**: "Tell them I'll be right down."   (Page 44)
               Black-out

EFFECTS PLOT

ACT I

Cue 1	**Doris**: "Thank you." *Front door slams*	(Page 4)
Cue 2	**Doris**: "…scrounged off the government to stay afloat." *Door intercom buzzer sounds*	(Page 8)
Cue 3	**Peggy**: "Goodbye, Mr Skinner." *Door intercom buzzer sounds*	(Page 11)
Cue 4	After pregnant pause between **Doris** and **Peggy** *Phone rings*	(Page 17)
Cue 5	**Doris**: "Oh God, *Wogan!*" *Distant car horn*	(Page 17)

ACT II

Cue 6	**Peggy** moves towards the phone *Door intercom buzzer sounds*	(Page 24)
Cue 7	**Doris**: "Nobody's coming to get you." *Door intercom buzzer sounds*	(Page 32)
Cue 8	**Sidney**: "…tonight your public will watch you die." *Door intercom buzzer sounds*	(Page 44)